Friends

Adjectives

1 **Put the words in order to make sentences.**

1 dark hair / has got / best friend / long / My

My best friend has got long dark hair.

2 hair / moustaches / and / spiky / They've / got

_____ .

3 sister / My / has got / hair / little / beautiful / curly

_____ .

4 has got / friend's / My / dad / is / but / he / a / bald / beard

_____ .

5 new / Our / good-looking / neighbour / really / is

_____ .

2 **Read. Then underline the adjectives.**

Alice is my best friend. She's so sporty! I'm the opposite; I'm lazy! I never do any sport. But I like watching sport on TV!

Alice is also very helpful and kind. If I can't do my homework, she always helps me. She does all her homework. She's clever and hard-working.

Her mum is very talkative! Every time I go to their house, she always asks me about everything I do and wants to hear all my news. She's not shy!

3 **Write the adjectives.**

1 He plays football every day. He's very s p o r t y .

2 She's a very warm and f ___ ___ ___ ___ ___ ___ ___ person.

3 She always thinks about other people. She's very k ___ ___ ___ .

4 It is h ___ ___ ___ ___ ___ ___ to talk to a friend when you have a problem.

5 Jake loves talking. He's not ___ ___ ___ !

4 **Find the self-portrait words.**

postimpressionismsharpabstractexpressionismdetail

1 _____ **2** _____

3 _____ **4** _____

5 **Read. Then match.**

1   What does she look like?

    a   She is intelligent and kind.

    b   She is Chinese.

    c   She has got blue eyes.

2   What does he look like?

    a   He likes cats.

    b   He's tall and he's got blond hair.

    c   He's funny and clever.

3   What do they look like?

    a   They are looking at the teacher.

    b   They like watching TV.

    c   They are good-looking.

4   What do you look like?

    a   I'm looking at a book.

    b   I've got dark hair and blue eyes.

    c   I like ice cream.

6 **Put the words in order to make questions. Then match.**

1   look / what / she / like / does

    What does she look like?

    a   He's small and thin.

2   like / you / do / what / look

    _____?

    b   My sister has got blue eyes.

3   sister / your / what / like / does / look

    _____?

    c   I've got blonde hair.

4   do / look / what / like / they

    _____?

    d   She's got long straight hair.

5   does / he / like / what / look

    _____?

    e   They are tall and thin.

7 **Read. Then answer the questions.**

1 What's he like?

He's clever and kind. _____ (clever / kind)

2 What's she like?

_____ (talkative / helpful)

3 What are they like?

_____ (hard-working / shy)

4 What's he like?

_____ (friendly / but / bossy)

5 What are you like?

_____ (sporty / clever)

8 **Look at the pictures. Write.**

1 bossy

2 shy / helpful

3 clever / hard-working

4 kind / friendly

5 sporty

1 She's bossy. She's got short grey hair. _____

2 _____ .

3 _____ .

4 _____ .

5 _____ .

9 **Put the words in order to make questions and answers.**

1 **A:** does / what / Tom / like / look

What does Tom look like?

B: got / spiky hair / he / has / blue eyes / and

_____ .

2 **A:** is / what / Kate / like

_____ ?

B: very / she / friendly / is / kind / and

_____ .

3 **A:** school / is / at / Joe / hard-working

_____ ?

B: is / hard-working / he / no, / at / but / home

_____ .

4 **A:** Lia / very / is / bossy

_____ ?

B: just / no, / is / she / talkative / very

_____ .

10 **Read and complete the sentences.**

| ~~beautiful~~ bossy kind clever helpful long brown talkative |

1 My best friend Sara is ____beautiful____ .

2 She's got _____ hair.

3 She is very _____ but a bit _____ .

4 She is _____ and always gets good marks in tests.

5 She is _____ – she sometimes helps me with my homework if I find it difficult.

6 I like her because she is _____ . She never stops talking!

11 **What makes a good friend? Write adjectives.**

I think a good friend is _____ .

12 **Look at the graph. Then read. What is a good friend like?**

_____ .

Describing a good friend — by Emily Bower

This graph shows what the children in my class think a good friend is like.

The answers are from thirteen children: six boys and seven girls. Here's what they think:

Eight children think a good friend is kind. They want a friend who tries to help people and make them happy.

Four children think a good friend is friendly. They like friends who like to meet new people. Only one person thinks that a good friend is clever with good marks in exams.

No one thinks that a 'bossy' person makes a good friend. They don't like someone telling them what to do all the time.

I agree with that! I think bossy people are very bad friends!

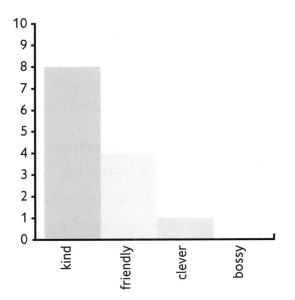

13 **Read the text again. Then circle *True* (T) or *False* (F).**

1 Seven children think a good friend is kind.   T / F

2 Most children think a good friend is bossy.   T / F

3 One child thinks a good friend is clever.   T / F

4 Four children think a good friend is friendly.   T / F

5 More children think a good friend is clever than bossy.   T / F

6 Emily thinks bossy people make good friends.   T / F

14 **Read the text again. Then complete.**

1 The graph _____ shows _____ what the children in Emily's class think
about what a _____ friend is like.

2 Four children think a good friend is _____.

3 Eight children think a good friend is _____.

4 No one thinks a _____ person makes a good friend.

5 Only one person thinks a good friend is _____.

15 **Read the text again. Then answer.**

1 How many boys are there in the class?   _____

2 How many girls are there in the class?   _____

3 Which adjective has got the highest number?   _____

4 Which adjective has got the lowest number?   _____

5 Which adjective has only got one vote?   _____

16 **Put the letters in order to make words. Then match with their opposites.**

1 sybso   a zaly

__ __ __ __ __   __ __ __ __

2 typsro   b ktevaliat

__ __ __ __ __ __   __ __ __ __ __ __ __ __ __

3 hsy   c dikn

__ __ __   __ __ __ __

17 Look at the graph. Then write about it.

- What does the graph show?
- Who are the answers from?
- What are their answers?
- Which adjective has got the highest/lowest number?
- Do you agree?

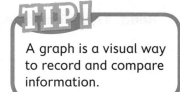

TIP!

A graph is a visual way to record and compare information.

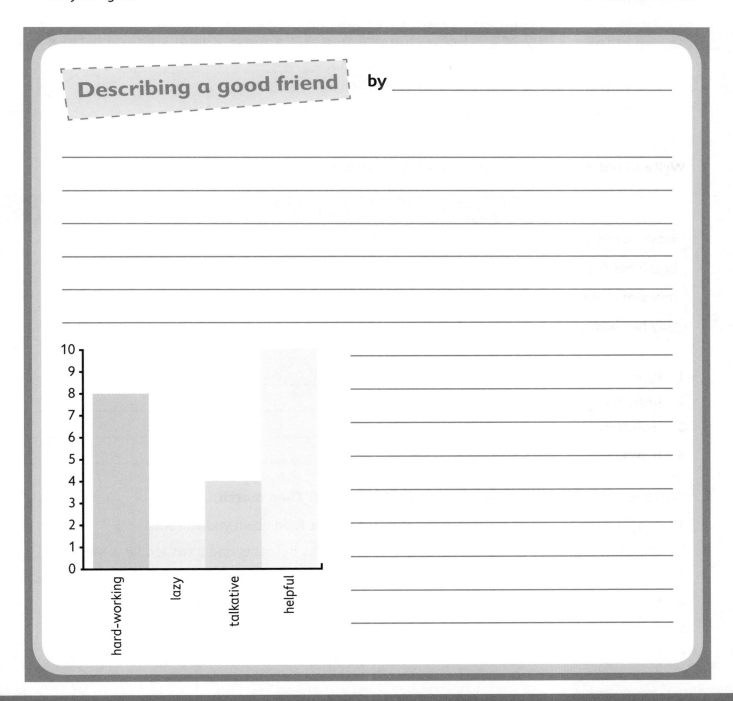

Describing a good friend by _____

2 My life
Daily routines

1 Read. Then complete.

a test   ~~my bed~~   my homework   out the rubbish   to bed early

18ᵗʰ March

I make ¹ __my bed__ before I go to school. I always help my parents take
² _____ . I never do ³ _____ when I get
home from school, but today I must revise for ⁴ _____ .
I'm very tired, so I should make sure that I go ⁵ _____ .

2 Write about Fiona. Use *always*, *usually*, *sometimes* and *never*.

	Monday	Tuesday	Wednesday	Thursday	Friday
wash her face	✔	✔	✔	✔	
brush her teeth	✔	✔	✔	✔	✔
make her bed					
tidy her bedroom				✔	✔

1 (always) Fiona always _____ .

2 (usually) _____

3 (sometimes) _____

4 (never) _____

3 Write *a, e, i, o* or *u* to complete the digestion words. Then match.

1 s __ l __ v __

2 st __ m __ ch

3 c __ l __ n

4 t __ ng __ __

5 w __ st __

6 l __ v __ r

a This pushes food down your throat.

b This absorbs nutrients and turns food into waste.

c This helps your intestine absorb nutrients and minerals.

d The place where your food gets broken down.

e This comes out of your body.

f Your mouth makes this and it helps you to chew.

4 **Read. Then match.**

1 I've got a test at 9 o'clock tomorrow.

2 My bedroom is a mess.

3 I want to help my mum.

4 I'm tired.

5 I don't know what homework to do.

6 I can't find my mobile.

a You should look under your bed!

b You should take notes in class.

c You should be on time.

d You should tidy it.

e You should take the rubbish out.

f You should brush your teeth and go to bed.

5 **Put the words in order to make sentences.**

1 remember / practise / to / must / piano / the / I

_____.

2 day / should / I / study / every

_____.

3 revise / Mark / must / English / for / test / the

_____.

4 for / must / not / lesson / he / late / his / be

_____.

2 I always do my homework

6 **Write sentences for you using adverbs of frequency.**

> sometimes   never   often   always   usually

1 I always tidy my room.

2 I _____ .

3 I _____ .

4 I _____ .

5 I _____ .

6 I _____ .

revise for a test

brush my teeth

tidy my room

do my homework

be on time

make my bed

wash my face

take notes in class

7 **What do you do? Read and complete.**

1 In the summer, I usually go to the beach with my family. _____

2 At the weekend, I always _____ .

3 On Wednesday afternoons, I often _____ .

4 First I _____ and then I _____ on Sundays.

5 Sometimes, I like to _____ in the morning.

6 I never eat _____ .

8 **Read. Then complete using the graph.**

I _____ usually get up _____ at seven o'clock.

I _____ at quarter to eight.

I _____ at eight o'clock,

before leaving for school.

At home, I _____ because

it's my brother who has to do it.

Finally, after dinner I _____ .

0 = never, 3 = sometimes,
4 = often, 5 = usually, 6 = always

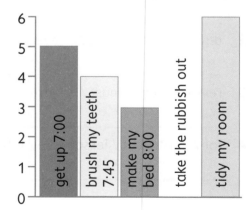

9 **Read. Then complete.**

~~should~~   finally   always   should   never   should   shouldn't   first

When you go shopping in a market you ¹_____should_____ always be careful.

Here is some advice. ²_____, you must always carry your bag in front

of you. ³_____ open your purse or wallet in the street to look for money.

You ⁴_____ try to look behind you when you are walking and you

⁵_____ stop to look at a map. ⁶_____ wear a money belt under

your coat to hide your money. Don't attract attention. ⁷_____, you shouldn't

wear expensive clothes or jewellery. Markets are great places to go shopping but

you ⁸_____ be careful!

10 **Look at the pictures. Then give advice. Use *always*.**

1   You should always _____.

2   _____.

3   _____.

4   _____.

11   **Do you get pocket money? How much? How often? Write.**

_____ .

12   **Read. What jobs can Tim do to get extra pocket money?**

_____ .

Tim's blog   Games   Music   Friends

In the UK, we usually get pocket money every week. Some of my friends sometimes get £1 a week. Others, like my friend Ben, always get £20! I get my pocket money on Saturdays. I never get £20 like Ben, but my parents always give me something. It's usually £5, but I sometimes get £10 or £15 if I do extra jobs!

This is the deal: when I do my homework, tidy my room and take the rubbish out after dinner every day, I can get an extra £1.50. That makes an extra £10.50 a week! That's a lot of money!

But sometimes when I get home from school, I'm really tired. The last thing I want to do is tidy my bedroom! And I never want to take the rubbish out. I hate taking the rubbish out!

So, every Saturday, I usually just get £5. I'm trying to save my pocket money to buy new trainers. Hopefully I won't be so tired next week so I can do my extra jobs and earn a bit more!

TIP!

Some parents give their children 'pocket money' – usually a small amount of money each week to spend on small items, or for children to start saving for something they want to buy.

13 **Read the text again. Then circle.**

1 Tim gets his pocket money on …

    a Fridays.

    b Saturdays.

    c Sundys.

2 Sometimes Tim doesn't tidy his room because he's …

    a lazy.

    b tired.

    c late for school.

3 Tim hates …

    a doing his homework.

    b making his bed.

    c taking the rubbish out.

14 **Read the text again. Then circle *True* (T) or *False* (F).**

1 Tim gets pocket money every week.   T / F

2 Ben's parents always give him £5 a week.   T / F

3 Tim is always tired when he gets home from school.   T / F

4 If Tim does all the jobs, he can get an extra £10.50.   T / F

5 Tim usually gets £15.50 on Saturdays.   T / F

15 **Match. Then find the words in Tim's blog and underline them.**

1 get   a the rubbish out

2 do   b pocket money

3 tidy   c extra jobs

4 take   d my room

16 **Read the answers. Then write questions about Tim.**

1 How often does Tim get pocket money?   Every week.

2 _____? On Saturday.

3 _____? Usually £5.

4 _____? He tidies his room, takes the rubbish out …

5 _____? When he gets home from school.

2 A blog entry

17 Underline seven more mistakes. Then correct.

During the week, I <u>gett</u> up at 7.30 a.m. to go to school. At the weekend I usualy get up at 9.00.

I somtimes read for an hour and then I lissen to music. After breckfast, we go to the supermarket

to get the shoping for the week. I alweys look at the magazines and meet my parents on the way

out. In the afternoon, I meet my frends and we play football. I love the weekend!

1 _____get_____   2 _____   3 _____

4 _____   5 _____   6 _____

7 _____   8 _____

18 Write a blog entry about pocket money.

- Do you get pocket money? (If not, use your imagination!).

- How much do you usually get?

- When do you usually get it?

- Do you have to do any jobs to get it? If yes, what jobs do you have to do?

- What do you usually do with your pocket money?

TIP!

A blog (short for Web Log) is a website where you can write information ordered by date.

Home   Blog   Games   Music   Friends

Free time

Hobbies and activities

1 **Write *a, e, i, o* or *u* to complete the words.**

1 r _e_ _a_ d _i_ ng p _o_ _e_ try

2 t __ ll __ ng j __ k __ s

3 d __ __ ng p __ zzl __ s

4 pl __ y __ ng ch __ ss

5 wr __ t __ ng st __ r __ __ s

6 m __ k __ ng m __ d __ ls

7 pl __ y __ ng th __ dr __ ms

2 **Look and write.**

1 playing computer games

2 d_____

3 r_____

4 r_____

5 s_____

k_____

6 a_____

3 **Put the letters in order to make ICT words.**

1 plouda   __ __ __ __ __ __

2 paps   __ __ __ __

3 onldwaod   __ __ __ __ __ __ __ __

4 neolin   __ __ __ __ __ __

5 slcoia demia   __ __ __ __ __ __ __ __ __ __ __

4 **Write sentences.**

1 Tom isn't good at catching. _____ (Tom / not good / catching)

2 _____ (Sam / good / throwing)

3 _____ (they / good / skateboarding)

4 _____ (we / not good / playing chess)

5 _____ (I / good / trampolining)

5 **Write questions. Then answer for yourself.**

1   What are you good at? _____

_____.

2   _____?

_____.

3   _____?

_____.

4   _____?

_____.

What were you doing yesterday?

6 Read. Then complete.

At 5 o'clock yesterday, I ¹_____was playing_____ (play) computer games. My little brother
²_____ (kick) a ball in the garden. My sister ³_____
(make) a model and my big brother ⁴_____ (read) a magazine.
My parents ⁵_____ (sing) karaoke with some friends.

7 Put the words in order to make questions. Then answer for yourself.

1 seven / you / o'clock / doing / were / yesterday / what / at / evening

What were you doing yesterday evening at seven o'clock?

I was _____.

2 watching / a / you / film / were / yesterday / afternoon

_____?

_____.

3 doing / were / your / what / friends / morning / at / eight / o'clock / this

_____?

_____.

4 your / races / were / running / yesterday / friends

_____?

_____.

5 were / school / to / Saturday / going / on / morning / they / eight / at / o'clock

_____?

_____.

6 parents / were / playing chess / this / your / o'clock / at / nine / morning

_____?

_____.

8 **Look at the table. Then write questions and answers.**

Yesterday	Tom	Sara
9:00	sleeping	playing football
11:00	playing computer games	trampolining
14:00	having lunch	having lunch
15:00	climbing trees	rollerblading

1 What was Tom doing at nine o'clock yesterday? _____ (Tom / 9:00)

He was sleeping. _____

2 _____? (Sara / 9:00)

_____.

3 _____? (Sara / 11:00)

_____.

4 _____? (Tom / 15:00)

_____.

5 _____? (Tom and Sara / 14:00)

_____.

9 **Read. Then circle.**

Tom: Are you good at ¹(*skateboard* / *skateboarding*)?

Sara: No, ²(*I'm* / *She's*) not good at skateboarding.

Tom: I'm not good ³(*at* / *in*) skateboarding either. I'd rather ⁴(*play* / *playing*) computer games
⁵(*than* / *in*) play sport!

Sara: I'm not good at ⁶(*playing* / *play*) computer games. I'd rather play sport!

10 **What do you like doing in your free time? Write.**

_____ .

11 **Read. What are the children writing about?**

_____ .

1

I'm Rob. In my free time I like playing football and volleyball. I often meet my friends after school and we play football in the park. My friends say I'm the best player in the school. I'm also captain of the school football team! I'm very good at playing sports but I also love watching them on TV — yesterday I was watching my favourite team on TV!

2

My name's Marcela and I love reading, so in my free time, I usually… read! I don't like watching TV or playing computer games. I also like going to the reading club at weekends — it's great fun! I'm also very good at writing — I want to write a book one day. Last night I was writing a short story for the school writing contest.

3

My name's Harry and I love music. I love listening to music, playing music and singing, of course! But I don't like dancing because I'm not very good at it. I play the drums and the piano. Next year I want to learn to play the guitar. At the weekend, my friends and I often sing karaoke. Music's great!

4

I'm Gwyneth and I do lots of things in my free time. I like drawing, watching TV, playing computer games and going shopping.

I often play computer games with my brother — he likes them, too. He also likes chess, but I don't because I'm not good at it. I never win! At the weekend I usually go shopping with my friend, Ann. Then, we usually have lunch together and in the afternoon we play computer games with my brother.

3 Describing interests and hobbies

12 Read the texts again. Then match.

1	Rob likes	a	music.
2	Marcela likes	b	computer games.
3	Harry likes	c	football.
4	Gwyneth likes	d	reading.

13 Read the texts again. Then circle.

1 Rob likes …
   a football and tennis.
   b tennis and volleyball.
   c football and volleyball.

2 Rob is captain of the school …
   a football team.
   b volleyball team.
   c basketball team.

3 Last night Marcela was writing a …
   a song.
   b story.
   c poem.

4 At the weekend, Gwyneth goes …
   a shopping.
   b singing.
   c dancing.

5 Gwyneth doesn't like …
   a drawing.
   b chess.
   c watching TV.

6 Harry plays …
   a the drums and the piano.
   b the guitar and the drums.
   c the piano and the guitar.

14 Read the texts again. Then answer.

1 Where do Rob and his friends often play football? _____.
2 What does Marcela want to do? _____.
3 What does Harry want to learn to play? _____.
4 When does Gwyneth usually go shopping? _____.

15 Look. Then match.

1	sing	a	music
2	play	b	the drums
3	have	c	lunch
4	listen to	d	karaoke
5	go	e	books
6	read	f	shopping

Describing interests and hobbies

Remember!

I like / love / enjoy / don't like **play**ing computer games.

I'm **good at** **playing computer games.**

16 **Write four things you like doing in your free time.**

_____

_____

_____

_____

17 **Write about your interests and hobbies.**

• What do you like doing in your free time?

• When / How often do you do these things?

• Who do you do them with?

• What are you good at?

_____

_____

_____

_____

_____

_____

_____

_____

_____

4 Around the world
Countries, places

1 Put the letters in order to make words. Then match.

1 tedser
___ ___ ___ ___ ___ ___

2 dyiprma
___ ___ ___ ___ ___ ___ ___

3 olovnca
___ ___ ___ ___ ___ ___ ___

a

b

c

d

e

f

4 ecav
___ ___ ___ ___

5 ytci
___ ___ ___ ___

6 etauts
___ ___ ___ ___ ___ ___

2 Put the letters in order to make eight countries. Remember to use capital letters!

1 teykur ___ ___ ___ ___ ___ ___

2 tepyg ___ ___ ___ ___ ___

3 aatulrsia ___ ___ ___ ___ ___ ___ ___ ___ ___

4 anringtea ___ ___ ___ ___ ___ ___ ___ ___ ___

5 cmieox ___ ___ ___ ___ ___ ___

6 cihan ___ ___ ___ ___ ___

7 padoln ___ ___ ___ ___ ___ ___

8 atiyl ___ ___ ___ ___ ___

3 Read. Then complete with the solar system words.

| forests | ~~air~~ | moon | lakes | planet | space |

19th August

I am in Argentina, in the Andes mountains. The 1 ____air____ is very clean and at night
you can see into 2 _____ really clearly. Often the 3 _____ is really bright.
There are lots of high mountains and 4 _____ where we can go fishing. There are lots of
5 _____ and animals here too. What an amazing place our 6 _____ is!

There isn't a ... / There aren't any ...

4 Put the words in order to make sentences.

1 there / any / in / aren't / Poland / crocodiles

<u>There aren't any crocodiles in Poland.</u>

2 Italy / a / there / rainforest / isn't / in

_____.

3 in / waterfall / is / a / there / Brazil

_____.

4 aren't / penguins / Spain / there / any / in

_____.

5 volcanoes / There / the / aren't / in / United Kingdom / any

_____.

6 there / beautiful / Australia / are / beaches / some / in

_____.

5 Read. Then write sentences.

1 hippos / Poland ✘

2 spiders / Australia ✔

3 mountains / Mexico ✔

4 Great Wall / Japan ✘

5 waterfalls / Egypt ✔

6 rainforest / Brazil ✔

1 <u>There aren't any hippos in Poland.</u>

2 _____.

3 _____.

4 _____.

5 _____.

6 _____.

4 Is there a ...? / Are there any ...?

6 Look at the picture. Then answer.

1 Are there any volcanoes?   No, there aren't.

2 Is there a dog in the sea?   _____.

3 Is there a monkey in the tree?   _____.

4 Are there any penguins?   _____.

5 Is there a boy throwing a ball?   _____.

7 Read. Then write the answers.

1 Is there a Sphinx statue in Egypt?   ✔ _____.

2 Is the River Nile in Colombia?   ✗ _____.

3 Are there any snowstorms in Greenland?   ✔ _____.

4 Is there a large ocean on Mars?   ✗ _____.

5 Is there a rainforest in Brazil?   ✔ _____.

8 Look. Then write questions.

1 Are there any lakes in Egypt?
  Yes, there are.

2 Is there _____?
  _____.

3 _____?
  _____.

4 _____?
  _____.

5 _____?
  _____.

6 _____?
  _____.

9 Read. Then answer the questions. Use short answers.

1 Is there a volcano in Italy?

Yes, there is. ✔

2 Are there any penguins in Egypt?

_____ ✗

3 Is there any water on Mars?

_____ ✔

4 Are there any mountains in London?

_____ ✗

5 Is there a big storm on Jupiter?

_____ ✔

6 Is there a statue in your school?

_____

10 Read. Then circle.

DO YOU NEED A HOLIDAY?

There ¹(*is* / *are*) so many places to visit.

What about visiting Greece?

There ²(*is* / *are*) a lot of islands to explore.

Or you could stay in Athens, the capital city. There ³(*is* / *are*) a lot of accommodation in this amazing city. There ⁴(*is* / *are*) some expensive hotels, but also a lot of cheap hotels.

There ⁵(*are* / *is*) a lot of different food to try. The seafood is delicious and there ⁶(*is* / *are*) a lot of very good fish restaurants.

And the beaches … There ⁷(*is* / *are*) so many beautiful beaches.

You must come to Greece!

11 **Do you write a diary about your trips?**

_____.

12 **Read. Then write. Where are the children?**

1 Mira _____.

2 Johnny _____.

3 Lucy _____.

Mira

My travel diary:
Colombia, South America

Friday, 14th June, Bogota

We are staying in a small hotel in Bogota. It's very warm. The people are very friendly and our rooms are very comfortable. Bogota is the capital of Colombia. It is in the Andes mountains. We can do lots of things here: we can go climbing, trekking and, of course, diving in the Caribbean. I can't wait! And the food is delicious — lots of seafood with hot spices. My favourite!

Sunday 6th May Cairo

My travel diary:
Egypt, Africa

I can't believe it – I'm in Egypt! I'm in Africa! I can see the River Nile from my window, but I can't see any crocodiles. There are lots of crocodiles in the Nile, so I can't go swimming. Tomorrow we're going to Alexandria. I'm so excited!

Johnny

My travel diary –
Greece, Europe

Tuesday, 14th August, Athens

Here I am in Greece! Wow! It's beautiful. The sea is so blue! I'm in a hotel in Athens, the capital of Greece. It's big and noisy!

Tomorrow we're going to Samos, one of the Greek islands. I can't wait! There are lots of beaches and small villages on the island. Our hotel is next to the beach. Three weeks of swimming – fantastic!

Lucy

13 Read the texts again. Then answer.

1 Who is going to Samos?

_____ .

2 Who can go diving in the Caribbean?

_____ .

3 Who is going to Alexandria?

_____ .

4 Who likes seafood?

_____ .

14 Read the texts again. Then match.

1 friendly people   a the River Nile

2 crocodiles   b Greece

3 islands   c Samos

4 small villages   d Bogota

15 Read the texts again. Then circle.

1 Mira thinks …

    a the food isn't very good.

    b the people are friendly.

    c Bogota is noisy.

2 Johnny is …

    a worried.

    b bored.

    c excited.

3 Tomorrow Lucy is going …

    a to a Greek island.

    b to Athens.

    c home.

4 Athens is …

    a big and noisy.

    b small and noisy.

    c small and quiet.

16 Read the texts again. Then write in the grid.

Colombia   crocodiles   Cairo   the Andes   spicy food   Samos   Egypt   swimming
Caribbean   Alexandria   Greece   River Nile   Bogota   Athens   noisy

South America	Africa	Europe
_____	_____	_____
_____	_____	_____
_____	_____	_____
_____	_____	_____

4   A travel diary entry

17 **Read and correct.**

    1 the river nile   _____

    2 the andes in colombia   _____

    3 the pyramids of egypt   _____

    4 samos in greece, europe _____

18 **Write your own travel diary.**

    • Where are you?

    • What is the country / city / town / island like?

    • Where are you staying?

    • What can you do / see there?

TIP!

You can use a diary to write about personal activities, ideas or feelings during a trip or holiday.

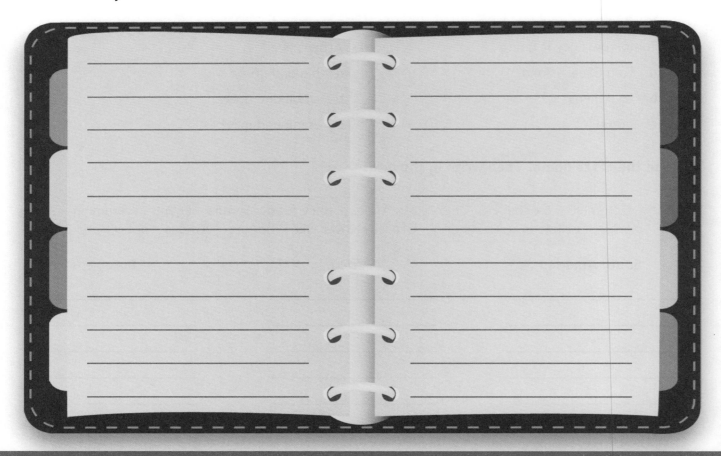

Shopping

5

Clothing and accessories, shopping

1 **Look at the pictures. Then write.**

1

___tracksuit___

2

_____

3

_____

4

_____

5

_____

6

_____

7

_____

8

_____

2 **Put the letters in order to make words. Then match the opposites.**

1 vinexesep ⎯ ⎯ ⎯ ⎯ ⎯ ⎯ ⎯ ⎯ ⎯

2 dol-hionfedsa ⎯ ⎯ ⎯ - ⎯ ⎯ ⎯ ⎯ ⎯ ⎯ ⎯ ⎯ ⎯

3 higtt ⎯ ⎯ ⎯ ⎯ ⎯

a baggy

b modern

c cheap

3 **Read. Then complete.**   receipt   change   department   coupons   community   customers

1 **A:** Here is your belt and your _____.

B: Oh, I gave you £5 and you didn't give me my _____!

2 **A:** Let's go shopping on Saturday.

B: Yes, let's go to that new _____ store!

3 **A:** There aren't enough shops in our _____.

B: No, there aren't. _____ need more variety!

4 **A:** Excuse me, can I use these _____ to pay for my shopping?

B: Yes, of course.

Is she going to ...? / Are you going to ...?

4 Look and make questions. Then answer.

1 she / sell ✔

Is she going to sell that watch? _____

Yes, she's going to sell that watch. _____

2 you / wear ✘

_____ ?

_____ .

3 they / buy ✔

_____ ?

_____ .

4 he / wear ✔

_____ ?

_____ .

5 Read. Then complete the dialogue.

| I'm | going | you | are | not |

Kate: What are you going to get Dad for his birthday? [1]_____ you going to buy that belt?

Sara: No, I'm [2]_____ going to buy that belt. It's too big. I'm [3]_____ to buy this black wallet.

Kate: That's a good idea. He needs a new wallet.

Sara: Are [4]_____ going to get him a present?

Kate: Yes, [5]_____ going to buy these gloves. Are they big enough?

Sara: Yes, they are. Great! Let's pay for them.

6 Read the answers. Then write the questions.

1 Whose jumper is this? _____ It's his jumper.

2 _____ ? They're Sue's trainers.

3 _____ ? It's my watch.

4 _____ ? They're William's books.

5 _____ ? They're Sara's glasses.

6 _____ ? It's Tom's tracksuit.

7 _____ ? It's Steph's bracelet.

8 _____ ? They're Maria's gloves.

7 Underline the mistakes. Then correct.

1 This sandwich is <u>my</u>.   This sandwich is mine. _____

2 These gloves are your.   _____ .

3 This ball is Tom.   _____ .

4 These kittens are her.   _____ .

5 This watch is him.   _____ .

6 These trousers are your.   _____ .

7 This hat is Sarah.   _____ .

8 Read. Then circle.

1 These flowers are mine.   These are (*mine* / *my*) flowers.

2 This book is his.   This is (*his* / *he*) book.

3 Those chips are hers.   Those are (*his* / *her*) chips.

4 These clothes are ours.   These are (*ours* / *our*) clothes.

5 This is their picture.   The picture is (*their* / *theirs*).

6 Those trousers are yours.   Those are (*you* / *your*) trousers.

7 That is her wallet.   That wallet is (*her* / *hers*).

9 **Find the mistakes. Then correct.**

1 Look at the sky! It's going rain!

Look at the sky! It's going to rain!

2 Are you to play football at the weekend?

_____ ?

3 This tracksuit is your.

_____ .

4 I going to see the latest Superman film tomorrow.

_____ .

5 These are Lisa gloves.

_____ !

10 **Read. Then circle.**

1
We're going on holiday!
I can't believe it! This afternoon we
(*are going to* / *go to*) pack our suitcases.
Here are (*our* / *ours*) clothes. Is this skirt
(*you* / *yours*), Kate?

2
No, it isn't (*me* / *mine*).

3
What about (*these* / *this*)
trainers. Are they
(*you* / *yours*)?

4
No, I don't think so.
I think they're (*Laura* /
Laura's).

5
This tracksuit is Johnny's.
And these trousers
are (*he* / *his*), too.

6
No, the trousers are (*my* / *mine*).
Do you like (*it* / *them*)?

11 **Where can you find adverts for clothes and accessories? Write.**

_____.

12 **Read. What do you think they should buy?**

_____.

Molly and John are twins. It's their birthday soon. They have asked for money for their birthday so they can go shopping for new things. Their mum and dad said they can spend up to £50 each.

They looked in some magazines and saw the following adverts. They are very excited. Some of the prices are too expensive but there are some good items that are cheap.

Molly wants some new clothes. She likes the pink tracksuit, but she also wants some jeans and a new shirt. John would rather have accessories. He likes the watch but it's too expensive. The wallet is a good price.

They work out how many things they can buy with their birthday money.

TRACKSUIT, pink, £40
For a girl 1.60 m tall
Photo on page 63
Tel: 775-846-5160, Amy

WALLET, new
Brown leather, only £20!
Tel: 563-558-9672
stephen-b@fdinternet.com

SHIRT, used, £5
White, baggy,
two pockets
For boys Size: small
Tel: 775-877-8800
Keith

GLOVES

3 pairs for £15
Red, green and black
Call Emma on 458-967-5894

JEANS, used, £10
Blue, tight
For girls; Size: medium
Photo on page 67
Tel: 699-856-4030, Rebecca
becky_smith@fdinternet.com

WATCH, new
Modern, black, for boys
Down from £150 to £65.50!
Call or email Fred   743-001-6644
fred_3451@ntdconline.com

UMBRELLA, new
Yellow, **£14**   Call Heather on 775-895-5550

13 Read the texts again. Then match.

1	pink	a	umbrella
2	brown	b	tracksuit
3	green	c	jeans
4	baggy	d	watch
5	modern	e	wallet
6	tight	f	gloves
7	yellow	g	shirt

14 Read the texts again. Then write the price of each.

1 watch _____

2 wallet _____

3 jeans _____

4 gloves (3 pairs) _____

5 umbrella _____

6 tracksuit _____

7 shirt _____

15 Read the texts again. Then circle.

1 The wallet is being sold by …

   a   Rebecca.

   b   Stephen.

   c   Fred.

3 Rebecca's jeans …

   a   are blue and tight.

   b   are red, green and black.

   c   are baggy.

5 Fred's watch is …

   a   used.

   b   new.

   c   a present for his mum.

2 Emma's gloves are …

   a   very colourful.

   b   in a different colour each pair.

   c   made from leather.

4 Keith is selling …

   a   an umbrella.

   b   a pair of gloves.

   c   a shirt.

6 Amy's tracksuit is …

   a   for a very tall girl.

   b   for a boy.

   c   for a girl 1.60 m tall.

Remember!

An advert is clear and simple. It only gives important information.

16 **Write eight things you have but don't need.**

_____

_____

_____

_____

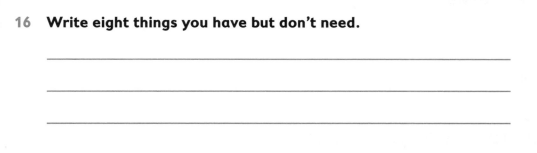

TIP!

An advert is a picture or words describing something that is for sale.

17 **Choose four things from Activity 16 and write adverts for them. Draw a picture for each one.**

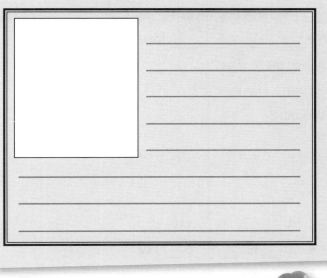

6 Party time

Irregular past tense verbs, celebrations

1 Read. Then complete.

> ate   brought   came   gave (x2)   had (x3)   made   met   sang

It was my friend Debbie's birthday yesterday. We all
[1] _____ in town at a pizza restaurant. Jake, Debbie's
cousin, [2] _____ with us, too. I [3] _____ a
present and a card for her. I [4] _____ her a beautiful pink
and white necklace. I [5] _____ the necklace myself!
Jake [6] _____ her a book. We [7] _____ lots
of food. I [8] _____ a four-cheese pizza. For
dessert, we all [9] _____ ice-cream. Then we
[10] _____ Happy Birthday! We all [11] _____
a really great time!

2 Write a, e, i, o or u to complete the words.

1 w _e_ dd _i_ ng

2 t ___ ___   p ___ rty

3 gr ___ d ___ ___ t ___ ___ n p ___ rty

4 d ___ nn ___ r p ___ rty

5 f ___ ncy dr ___ ss p ___ rty

6 s ___ rpr ___ s ___   p ___ rty

7 f ___ r ___ w ___ ll p ___ rty

8 p ___ cn ___ c

3 Put the letters in order to make the history words.

1 tivear ecasniamr   N _a_ _t_ _i_ _v_ _e_ A _m_ _e_ _r_ _i_ _c_ _a_ _n_ _s_

2 serseltt   s _ _ _ _ _ _ _

3 gevoya   v _ _ _ _ _

4 tedcelebra   c _ _ _ _ _ _ _ _ _

5 dkaned   l _ _ _ _ _

6 ssecrod   c _ _ _ _ _ _

7 tomnhs   m _ _ _ _ _

4 Read. Then complete the tables.

Present		Past
make	**1**	made
3		had
come	**5**	
7		could
eat	**9**	

Present		Past
give	**2**	
bring	**4**	
6		met
see	**8**	
10		went

5 Read. Then complete using the past tense.

When I was seven, I ¹___could___ (can) play the piano a little. I ²_____ (have) a really

good piano teacher. She ³_____ (be) very kind and ⁴_____ (help) me to learn

a lot. I ⁵_____ (play) in front of my school. That ⁶_____ (be) great.

I ⁷_____ (get) really excited. All my family ⁸_____ (come) to watch me.

Then my class ⁹_____ (sing) two of my favourite songs. I ¹⁰_____ (win)

a prize for my performance!

Now, I'm twelve. Last term, I ¹¹_____ (start) to learn to bake. I love baking cakes.

It's quite difficult, but I ¹²_____ (make) a cake every week for the first month.

And I ¹³_____ (take) my cakes to my Grandma's house for her to try. At school last

week, we ¹⁴_____ (have) a charity event and I ¹⁵_____ (bring) my cakes to sell.

I think we ¹⁶_____ (make) a lot of money!

6 **Put the words in order to make questions. Then answer for yourself.**

1 you / year / holiday / where / on / did / go / last

Where did you go on holiday last year?

_____ .

2 go / did / with / you / who

_____ ?

_____ .

3 did / who / meet / you

_____ ?

_____ .

4 do / did / what / you

_____ ?

_____ .

5 you / what / see / did

_____ ?

_____ .

6 type / of / did / what / food / eat / you

_____ ?

_____ .

7 **Match.**

1	where	**a**	Jill
2	when	**b**	the party
3	why	**c**	a present
4	who	**d**	yesterday
5	what	**e**	It was her birthday.

8 **Write sentences.**

1 I / eat / a pizza ✗ // eat / a hamburger ✔   I didn't eat a pizza, I ate a hamburger.

2 he / come / today ✗ // come / yesterday ✔   _____ .

3 we / go / Spain ✗ // go / Argentina ✔   _____ .

4 she / meet / Tom ✗ // meet / me ✔   _____ .

5 they / see / giraffe ✗ // see / hippo ✔   _____ .

9 **Put the words in order to make sentences and questions.**

1 present / he / my / brought / a / to / party

He brought a present to my party.

2 did / film / why / like / she / the

_____?

3 party / twins / the / go / to / the / couldn't

_____.

4 meet / you / party / did / who / the /at

_____?

5 when / see / film / the / did / you

_____?

6 one / my / walk / when / sister / could / she / was

_____.

10 **Read. Then rewrite in the opposite form.**

1 We *saw* the film yesterday.

We didn't see the film yesterday.

2 I *could play* the violin last year.

_____.

3 He *didn't watch* TV yesterday evening.

_____.

4 My friends *came* to my house yesterday.

_____.

5 We *didn't meet* Tom and Sara after school.

_____.

6 She *made* a cake for his birthday yesterday afternoon.

_____.

11 **Do you like parties? Why? / Why not? Write.**

_____ .

12 **Read. Then write. When was the party?**

_____ .

send   save   discard

To: elena.taylor@mymail.com

From: eejameson@free.net

Hi Elena,

How are you? I hope you and your family are well.

I had such a fantastic time last weekend! My friend Lizzie passed all her exams. Her parents were so happy. They wanted to do something special for her as a surprise, so they organised a pool party at the sports centre.

My brother and I helped. I wrote the invites and he blew up the balloons. My mum made an amazing chocolate cake. Lizzie's dad loves barbecues, so he was outside cooking sausages, beef burgers and chicken kebabs. He also made some veggie burgers and vegetable kebabs because some of our friends don't eat meat – they're vegetarians. And we had jacket potatoes (we sometimes call them baked potatoes), too. They're my favourite!

Later we played water volleyball in the pool with a plastic ball. That was great fun! I'm going to work really hard for my exams. Then I can have a party, and you can come, too!

Okay, that's all my news. Write soon and tell me your news.

Love,
Emily

13 Read the text again. Then match.

1 Emily   a   made a chocolate cake.

2 Emily's mum   b   passed her exams.

3 Emily's brother   c   loves jacket potatoes.

4 Lizzie's parents   d   blew up balloons.

5 Lizzie's dad   e   loves barbecues.

6 Lizzie   f   organised the surprise party.

14 Read the text again. Then circle.

1 Emily is writing to …

    a   a friend.

    b   someone she doesn't know.

    c   her grandmother.

2 Lizzie's parents organised the party because …

    a   it was Lizzie's birthday.

    b   Lizzie loves parties.

    c   Lizzie passed her exams.

3 The party was …

    a   in the garden.

    b   at the sports centre.

    c   at Lizzie's house.

4 Emily wants to work hard for her exams because …

    a   she wants to see Elena.

    b   she wants a party like Lizzie's.

    c   she loves jacket potatoes.

15 Read the text again. Then circle *True* (T) or *False* (F).

1 Emily's brother helped, too.   T / F

2 Emily's mum made some ice cream.   T / F

3 All of Lizzie and Emily's friends eat meat.   T / F

4 Emily played water volleyball at the party.   T / F

16 Read the text again. Then answer.

1 Who did Emily write the email to?

Emily wrote the email to her friend, Elena.

2 Where did they play water volleyball?

_____ .

3 What did the vegetarians eat?

_____ .

4 How did Emily and her brother help with the party?

_____ .

6 An email

17 Write an email to a friend about a party you had.

- When / Where was the party?
- Why did you have the party?
- Who came?
- What did you do?

- What did you have to eat?
- How was the food?
- Did you have a good time?

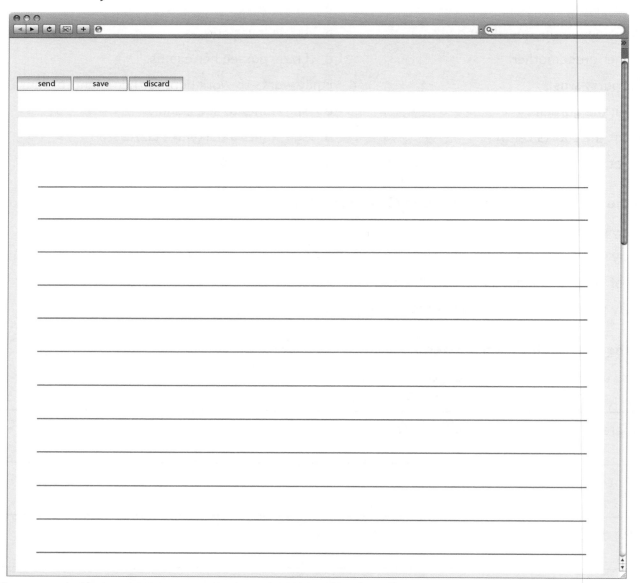

Adjectives, school, the flu

1 Put the letters in order to make words. Then match the opposites.

1 igobrn   __ __ __ __ __ __   a funny

2 liftifcdu   __ __ __ __ __ __ __ __ __   b interesting

3 ayrcs   __ __ __ __ __   c easy

2 Write the school subjects.

1

2

3

_____

_____

_____

4

5

6

_____

_____

_____

3 Read. Then match.

1 The flu   a if you have the flu.

2 Coughing and sneezing   b through coughing.

3 Stay at home   c are symptoms of the flu.

4 Germs can spread   d is a virus.

4 **Put the words in order to make questions. Then answer for yourself.**

1 any / homework / was / yesterday / Maths / there

Was there any Maths homework yesterday? _____

_____ .

2 computers / class / were / in / there / any / yesterday

_____ ?

_____ .

3 interesting / your / was / class / last

_____ ?

_____ .

4 to / school / you / late / yesterday / were

_____ ?

_____ .

5 **Write questions and answers.**

1 Was the film funny? _____ (film / funny)

No, it wasn't. _____ ✘

2 _____? (poem / boring)

_____ . ✔

3 _____? (school lessons / difficult)

_____ . ✘

4 _____? (homework / easy)

_____ . ✘

5 _____? (book / interesting)

_____ . ✔

6 Read. Then match.

1 Did you go to bed early last night?
2 Did you read the Harry Potter books in English?
3 Did you go to school last week?
4 Did you eat all the vegetables?
5 Did you see the Batman film?

a No, I didn't. I was ill.
b No, I didn't. I ate the meat.
c Yes, I did. I went to bed at 7 o'clock.
d No, I didn't. They're too long!
e No, we didn't. We saw Superman.

7 Read the answers. Then write suitable questions.

1 Did you go to England last year?

No, I didn't. I went to Italy.

2 _____ ?

No, I didn't. But I saw lots of frogs and small lizards.

3 _____ ?

No, I didn't. I stayed at home and read a comic.

4 _____ ?

No, I didn't. I studied English.

8 Put the words in order to make questions.

1 the / scary / film / did / have / alien / it / in / an

Did the scary film have an alien in it?

2 Maths / Maddy / did / homework / Monday / on / have

_____ ?

3 did / today / go / to / you / football practice

_____ ?

4 last / night / you / did / your / homework / finish

_____ ?

9 Read. Then answer the questions.

1 Did you go to the cinema last week?   <u>No, I didn't.</u> ✗

2 Was it your birthday yesterday?   _____. ✔

3 Were there any children at school yesterday?   _____. ✗

4 Were there any good presents at the party?   _____. ✔

5 Did they sing good songs?   _____. ✗

6 Was there any homework yesterday?   _____. ✔

10 Read. Then complete.

1 ____Did____ you see a film yesterday?

Yes, I 2_____. It 3_____ interesting!

4_____ it funny?

No, 5_____ was exciting.

6_____ there any children in the film?

No, there weren't, but there 7_____ aliens!

It sounds scary!

It was! Did 8_____ go swimming yesterday?

No, we 9_____.
We 10_____ skateboarding.
It was really hard!

11 Read. Then complete.

1 ____Did____ you _____ (finish) your lunch?

2 _____ it _____ (rain) yesterday?

3 _____ she _____ (help) her mum?

4 _____ they _____ (study) English yesterday?

12 Have you got rules at your school? What are they?

_____

_____.

13 Read. Does Maria think school rules are a good thing? What do you think?

_____

_____.

Are school rules a good thing?

In my school we have lots of rules and I think this is how it should be. Firstly, there are usually a lot of children in a school. In some countries, there are often over thirty children in a class. In other countries, there are over a hundred children in a class. It's important to have some rules so that everyone can work together safely. For example, going from one classroom to another or going up and down the stairs.

Secondly, rules help us to learn more about life outside school. We learn subjects like Maths, Music, Geography and Science, but we also learn what we can and can't do. This is interesting too! We learn how to talk to different people and to respect their ideas. We also learn what happens if we do something we shouldn't do!

Thirdly, rules help us to work and learn how to do things in a specific period of time. They help us to organise our lives so there is time to work and to relax. Sometimes the lesson takes longer because someone is talking or playing around. I don't think this is helpful for anyone!

In conclusion, I think rules are a good thing. What do you think? What rules do you have in your school? Do you think there should be more rules or fewer rules in your school?

TIP!

- When you write an argument, you present your ideas about something in a convincing way.
- A paragraph is a collection of lines about the same idea. We use them to present our ideas clearly.

14 Read the text again and find the main ideas. Then match.

1 First paragraph   a Learning to respect other ideas

2 Second paragraph   b Helping to organise our lives

3 Third paragraph   c Working together

15 Read the text. Then circle.

1 Maria thinks rules are good for …

   a helping people.

   b making classrooms quiet.

   c keeping the classroom and school safe.

3 Maria thinks lessons take longer when …

   a there are no rules.

   b some children aren't working.

   c the class gets extra homework.

2 In some countries, there are …

   a more than a hundred children in a class.

   b fewer than thirty children in a class.

   c thirty classes in one school.

4 Maria thinks it's good to organise our lives …

   a so we can have longer lessons.

   b so we can work together safely.

   c so we have time to work and to relax.

16 Find the words or expressions in the text for these descriptions.

1 These help you to organise your life.

   _____

3 The opposite of inside.

   _____

2 Where you attend lessons in school.

   _____

4 You sometimes use a calculator for this subject.

   _____

17 Read the text again. Then answer.

1 How can people work together safely?

   People can work together safely by having rules.

2 What does Maria think is interesting?

   _____.

3 Do rules help us with our time?

   _____.

4 What does Maria think is not helpful for anyone?

   _____.

Start a new paragraph for every new idea.

18 **Write about rules in your school / home.**

- What are the rules in your school / home?

- Why do you think there are these rules?

- Do you think they are good or bad?

- What other rules can you make?

8 All about us
Nationalities, occupations, inventions

1 Write (✔) or (✗). Then correct.

1 Argeninian ✗ _____Argentinian_____

2 Mexican ☐ _____

3 Astralian ☐ _____

4 South Corean ☐ _____

5 Pollish ☐ _____

6 Spanish ☐ _____

2 Look at the pictures. Then write the jobs.

1 _____

2 _____

3 _____

3 Read. Then write.

1 A woman who works in business. __ u __ __ __ __ __ __ __ __ __ __ __ __

2 Someone who is interested in science. __ __ i __ __ __ __ __ __ __

3 Someone who works on the sea. __ __ __ __ o __

4 Someone who works with cars. __ __ __ __ h __ __ __ __ __

5 Someone who stars in films. __ c __ __ __ __

6 Someone who plays a musical instrument. __ __ s __ __ __ __ __

4 Write *a*, *e*, *i*, *o* or *u* to complete the words about inventions.

1 __ nv __ nt __ r

2 d __ s __ gn __ d

3 c __ nstr __ ct __ d

4 cr __ __ t __ d

5 __ d __ __

5 Read. Then write.

1 I come from South Korea.   I'm South Korean.

2 We come from China.   _____.

3 They come from Egypt.   _____.

4 He comes from Japan.   _____.

5 She comes from Turkey.   _____.

6 Read. Then complete.

1 Hi there! I'm Jaime. I'm from Spain. I'm _____. These are my friends.

2 Caterina is from Italy. She's _____.

3 Luiz is from Brazil. He's _____.

4 Monika and Anna are from _____. They are Polish.

5 And Simon is from _____. He's British.

7 Put the words in order to make conversations.

1 you / are / where / from

A: Where are you from? _____

Mexico / I'm / from

B: _____.

2 from / are / Argentina / they

A: _____?

they / yes, / Argentinian / are

B: _____.

3 are / Mexico / from / you

A: _____?

no, / Spain / I'm / from

B: _____.

A friend who ... / A car that ...

8 **Read. Then write sentences.**

1 She is a girl from school. She helped me carry my suitcase.
   She is the girl from school who helped me carry my suitcase.

2 He is a teacher. He teaches P.E.

   _____.

3 Karen is my friend. She beat me in the tennis match!

   _____.

4 They are film stars. They were in the park.

   _____.

5 They are Australians. They taught me how to surf.

   _____.

9 **Look at the flags and complete. Then write sentences using *who* or *that*.**

1 This is a popular ball game. It comes from Spain.
   This is a popular ball game that comes from Spain.

2 She's an _____ singer. She sings all over the world.

   _____.

3 This is a car. It is made in _____.

   _____.

4 These are computers. They were made in _____.

   _____.

5 He's a famous businessman. He's from _____.

   _____.

10 **Read. Then circle.**

1 This is the swimming pool (*where* / *who*) I go swimming before school.

2 These are the friends (*which* / *who*) play with me.

3 Those are the presents (*where* / *which*) I got for my birthday.

4 That is the song (*where* / *which*) I've got to learn.

5 She is the aunt (*which* / *who*) takes me ice skating.

6 That is the place (*which* / *where*) I play volleyball.

11 **Read and write the quiz questions using *who* or *which*. Then answer.**

1. This is a city. It is the capital of Argentina.
This is a city which is the capital of Argentina.
Buenos Aires

2. This is a special celebration. It's celebrated on the 25th of December.
_____ .
_____

3. This is an important person in Great Britain. She lives in Buckingham Palace.
_____ .
_____

4. This is a famous character in a book. He is a young magician.
_____ .
_____

5. This is a famous festival. It's celebrated on the last day of October.
_____ .
_____

12   **In your country, do you have special days to celebrate different cultures? What do you do? Write.**

_____

_____ .

13   **Read. What is the text about?**

_____ .

Egypt

Argentina

Brazil

Great Britain

China

International Day

One of the best days of the school year is International Day. It's a really special day because there are lots of exciting events for everyone in the school. A lot of nationalities from all over the world are present.

This year, International Day was on the 3rd of February. Each class had a country and all the children in that class — with their parents and teachers — worked together to decorate their classroom with pictures and maps from different countries (Brazil, Colombia, Egypt, Japan, ...) and posters of important people from that country (astronauts, footballers, painters ...). Other rooms had displays of traditional costumes and showed DVDs of national dances. In the main hall, there were typical foods: Chinese, Spanish, Australian ...

The younger children had a special passport. They took this to each classroom and had to find out information about the country. Then they got a special stamp in their passport. There was a prize for the passport with the most stamps. There were also more prizes. The first prize was a trip for two people to Canada!

The day ended with a concert with students, teachers and parents singing a song or playing musical instruments from 'their' country. It was amazing!

Italy

14 **Read the text again. Then circle.**

1 International Day is special because …

    a there are different kinds of food.

    b there are special events.

    c it's in February.

2 The food was in the …

    a classrooms.

    b playground.

    c hall.

3 The younger children's passport had …

    a space for special stamps to go in it.

    b questions for the children to answer.

    c lots of pictures.

4 At the end of the day, teachers and parents …

    a sang or played musical instruments.

    b played games.

    c decorated the classrooms.

15 **Read the text again. Then circle *True* (T) or *False* (F).**

1 Younger students never take part in the events.   T / F

2 There were maps in the main hall.   T / F

3 There was food from many different countries.   T / F

4 All the children had a passport.   T / F

5 There were pictures in the classrooms.   T / F

6 The last activity was the concert.   T / F

16 **Match. Then find these words in the text and underline them.**

1 special   **a** costumes

2 traditional   **b** instruments

3 first   **c** passport

4 musical   **d** prize

17 **Read the answers. Then write suitable questions.**

1 Why is it a really special day? _____

Because there are lots of exciting events.

2 _____?

The children, teachers and parents.

3 _____?

On the 3rd February.

4 _____?

In the main hall.

5 _____?

They had a special passport.

6 _____?

The first prize was a trip for two to Canada.

8 A school magazine article

18 **Write about a special celebration at your school.**

- What is the celebration?
- Why do you have this celebration?
- What do you do?
- What do you eat?